It's Laugh o'clock
Would you Rather?
Eww! Edition

Funny Scenarios, Wacky Choices
and Hilarious Situations
for Kids and Family

With Fun Illustrations

Riddleland

Copyright 2021 - Riddleland All rights reserved.

The content contained within this book may not be reproduced, duplicated or transmitted without direct written permission from the author or the publisher.

By reading this document, the reader agrees that under no circumstances is the author responsible for any losses, direct or indirect, that are incurred as a result of the use of the information contained within this document, including, but not limited to, errors, omissions, or inaccuracies.

Legal Notice:
This book is copyright protected. It is only for personal use. You cannot amend, distribute, sell, use, quote or paraphrase any part, or the content within this book, without the consent of the author or publisher.

Disclaimer Notice:
Please note the information contained within this document is for educational and entertainment purposes only. All effort has been executed to present accurate, up to date, reliable, complete information. No warranties of any kind are declared or implied. Readers acknowledge that the author is not engaged in the rendering of legal, financial, medical or professional advice. The content within this book has been derived from various sources. Please consult a licensed professional before attempting any techniques outlined in this book.

Designs by freepik.com

TABLE OF CONTENTS

Introduction — pg 5

Turn it into a game — pg 7

Would You Rather? — pg 9

Did you enjoy the book? — pg 109

Bonus Book — pg 110

Contest — pg 111

Other books by Riddleland — pg 112

About Riddleland — pg 114

Riddleland Bonus

Join our **Facebook Group** at **Riddleland for Kids**
to get daily jokes and riddles.

• • • • • • • • • • • • • • • • • • •

https://pixelfy.me/riddlelandbonus

Thank you for buying this book. As a token of our appreciation, we would like to offer a special bonus—a collection of 50 original jokes, riddles, and funny stories.

INTRODUCTION

"People say love is the best feeling, but I think finding a toilet when you are having diarrhea is better."

~ Unknown

Are you ready to make some decisions? **It's Laugh O'Clock - Would You Rather? Eww! Edition** is a collection of funny scenarios, wacky choices, and hilarious situations which offer alternative endings for kids and adults to choose among.

These questions are an excellent way to get a fun and exciting conversation started. Also, by asking "Why?" after a "Would you Rather . . . " question, learn a lot about the person, including their values and their thinking process.

We wrote this book because we want children to be encouraged to read more, think, and grow. As parents, we know that when children play games, they are being educated while having so much fun that they don't even realize they're learning and developing valuable life skills. "Would you Rather . . . " is one of our favorite games to play as a family. Some of the 'would you rather ...' scenarios have had us in fits of giggles, others have generated reactions such as: "Eeeeeeuuugh, that's gross!," and yet others really make us think, reflect and consider our own decisions.

Besides having fun, playing these questions have other benefits such as:

Enhancing Communication – This game helps children to interact, read aloud, and listen to others. It's a fun way for parents to get their children interacting with them without a formal, awkward conversation. The game can also help to get to know someone better and learn about their likes, dislikes, and values.

Building Confidence – The game encourages children to get used to pronouncing vocabulary, asking questions, and overcoming shyness.

Developing Critical Thinking – It helps children to defend and justify the rationale for their choices and can generate discussions and debates. Parents playing this game with young children can give them prompting questions about their answers to help them reach logical and sensible decisions.

Improving Vocabulary – Children will be introduced to new words in the questions, and the context of them will help them remember the words because the game is fun.

Encouraging Equality and Diversity – Considering other people's answers, even if they differ from your own, is important for respect, equality, diversity, tolerance, acceptance, and inclusivity. Some questions may get children to think outside the box and move beyond stereotypes associated with gender.

Welcome to It's Laugh O'Clock

Would You Rather?
Eww! Edition

How do you play?

At least two players are needed to play this game. Face your opponent and decide who is **Stinky Sock 1** and **Stinky Sock 2**. If you have 3 or 4 players, you can decide which players belong to **Stinky Sock Group 1** and **Stinky Sock Group 2**. The goal of the game is to score points by making the other players laugh. The first player to reach a score of 10 points is the **Round Champion**.

What are the rules?

Stinky Sock 1 starts first. Read the questions aloud and choose an answer. The same player will then explain why they chose the answer in the silliest and wackiest way possible. If the reason makes the Stinky Sock 2 laugh, then Stinky Sock 1 scores a funny point. Take turns going back and forth and write down the score.

If you have three or four players

Flip a coin. The Stinky Sock that guesses it correctly starts first.

> **Bonus Tip:**
> Making funny voices, silly dance moves or wacky facial expressions will make your opponent laugh!

> Most Importantly:
> **Remember to have fun and enjoy the game!**

Would You Rather...

Wear smelly socks you can't take off

OR

walk barefoot in a muddy, sloppy pig pen?

Use a toilet with hissing snakes in it

OR

use the bathroom after the abominable snowman used it?

Would You Rather...

Sleep in a barn with a family of pigs

OR

never sleep at all?

Lick the floor with your tongue

OR

shampoo your hair with someone else's spit?

Would You Rather...

Eat dog food

OR

fresh kitty litter?

• •

Go to school for a day naked

OR

eat a healthy leafy green spinach salad
for lunch every day all week?

Would You Rather...

Wake up completely bald one day

OR

wake up with your body covered in orange fuzzy orangutan fur?

• • • • • • • • • • • • • • • • • • • •

Have flakes fall from your hair like a snow-shower every time you sneeze

OR

have boogers come out of your nose whenever you talk?

12

Would You Rather...

Take a bath in toilet water once

OR

never be able to take a bath?

• • • • • • • • • • • • • • •

Chew someone else's toenails

OR

eat gum you found under a bench in the park?

Would You Rather...

Wash your hands in the toilet

OR

never be able to wash them again?

"Water here ♡"

Rinse your mouth with dish soap

OR

drink water from the washing machine?

Would You Rather...

Drink dirty dishwater

OR

drink after someone spits in your water bottle?

Smell someone else's feet

OR

eat their boogers?

Would You Rather...

Drink rotten milk

OR

dirty water after washing a car?

This is for you.

• • • • • • • • • • • • • • • • •

Take a nap the sidewalk of a busy street

OR

Hug your house's toilet bowl?

Would You Rather...

Pick your nose in public

🔄 OR 🔄

someone else's in private?

• • • • • • • • • • • • • • • • • • • •

Only be able to eat other people's leftovers

🔄 OR 🔄

never be able to finish a meal?

Would You Rather...

Sleep in a smelly dirty trash can

OR

on a wet bed every night?

• •

Have healthy green colored teeth

OR

white teeth that have painful cavities?

Would You Rather...

Eat a moldy chocolate chip cookie

OR

eat a piece of chocolate cake that fell in a mud puddle?

• •

Change a baby's stinky dirty diaper

OR

have them barf warm puke on you?

Would You Rather...

Wear shoes that smell super sweaty

OR

shoes that pinch your toes together because they're a size too small?

• •

Have slimy worms crawling in your bed while you're sleeping

OR

take a shower with a tub full of slippery snakes?

Would You Rather...

Eat cookies with worm poop in them

OR

a cake with rotten eggs in it?

• • • • • • • • • • • • • • • • • • •

Lose all of your hair

OR

have a head full of creepy-crawly lice?

Would You Rather...

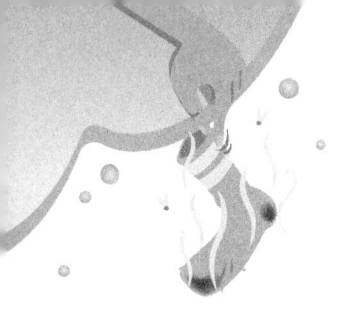

Drink a glassful of raw eggs

OR

eat the smelliest fruit in the world, durian?

• •

Wipe the sweat off your friend's forehead with your hand

OR

wear their super sweaty baseball cap?

Would You Rather...

Eat raw meat you can see

OR

let someone else feed you any food they want while you are blindfolded?

• •

Sleep in a bed of quicksand

OR

on a bed with nails sticking up in it?

Would You Rather...

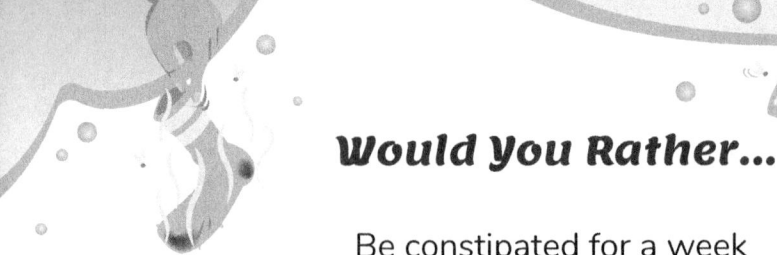

Be constipated for a week

OR

have diarrhea for three whole days?

• • • • • • • • • • • • • • • •

Be a dog that eats its own puke

OR

a cat that constantly coughs out hairballs?

Would You Rather...

Eat toothpaste for the rest of your life

OR

never brush your teeth again and have bad breath?

Drink a cockroach milkshake

OR

a cup of hot chocolate with dead flies floating in it instead of marshmallows?

Would You Rather...

Find a spider as big as your hand on your pillow

OR

have a shoe full of grasshoppers?

• •

Be tickled by all eight arms of an octopus

OR

have ten fish nibbling at the skin on your feet all at once?

Would You Rather...

Sit naked in the sun for a week

OR

sit in dirty water for a day?

• •

Sleep outside in the open for a month

OR

not be able to change the clothes you are wearing for two weeks?

Would You Rather...

Eat earwax from someone else's ear

OR

eat the earwax from your own ear?

Here, my earwax!

• • • • • • • • • • • • • • •

Have your friend sneeze in your ear

OR

cough into your mouth?

Would You Rather...

Have one eye in the middle of your forehead

OR

have your mouth under the hair on the back of your head?

• • • • • • • • • • • • • • •

Play in a sandbox full of biting ants

OR

swim in a pool full of stinging jellyfish?

Would You Rather...

Take a big sniff of your friend's sweaty hair

OR

a big whiff from their sweaty armpit?

• •

Have rotten egg burps

OR

dirty diaper flavored hiccups?

Would You Rather...

Get trapped in a small closet full of smelly shoes

OR

get trapped in a creepy dark attic full of swooping bats?

Eat pizza covered with tons and tons of spinach

OR

eat a cake frosted with mashed cauliflower?

Would You Rather...

Have itchy mosquito bites all over your body that no one can see

OR

big red pimples filled with oozy white stuff all over your face?

• • • • • • • • • • • • • • • • • • • •

Eat a cockroach in a hot dog bun

OR

a mud pie in a hamburger bun?

Would You Rather...

Have a sleepover with a friend who has terrible breath

OR

a friend who has smelly farts?

Ride in a bus full of sweaty people

OR

sit on a seat that someone just peed on?

Would You Rather...

Wear someone else's day old dirty underwear

OR

not change your underwear for a week?

Eat food licked by a dog

OR

food that has been dropped on the ground?

Would You Rather...

Clean a cat's litter box with your hands

OR

spread butter made from mashed worms on everything you eat?

• •

Play hide and seek in a circus full of creepy clowns

OR

in a haunted house?

Would You Rather...

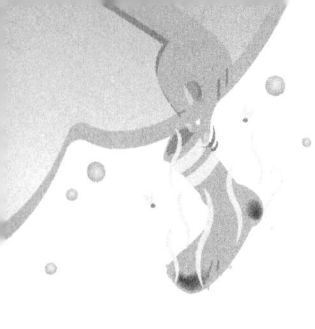

Have a two-headed teacher

OR

a big piece of chewed gum on your desk chair?

Wear a shirt with a big chocolate stain on it

OR

have a big piece of hair sticking right out of your head in your school pictures?

Would You Rather...

Eat cereal with rotten milk

OR

toast covered in jelly and ants for breakfast?

Go down a slide after someone puked on it

OR

sit in your desk after someone peed their pants?

Would You Rather...

Drip sweat all day long

OR

have greasy hair?

- - - - - - - - - - - - -

Swim 200 meters in a tank full of sharks

OR

swim in a tank full of dead fish?

Would You Rather...

Have to eat your whole math book for lunch

OR

drink a milkshake made from sweaty gym socks?

• •

Ride a bike that has to be powered by your farts

OR

on a skateboard that is a giant taste bud covered tongue?

Would You Rather...

Lick your cat's paws

OR

lick your smelly sweaty feet?

• •

Have to eat worms fed to you by a bird

OR

chewed up food spit into your mouth by your mom?

Would You Rather...

Eat a dead bug

OR

a live worm?

- - - - - - - - - - - - - - -

Eat pizza made with stinky cheese

OR

popcorn sprinkled with fried ants?

Would You Rather...

Eat a handful of sand

OR

wear shoes that are always full of sand?

Turn into a zombie with only one arm

OR

have one of your eyeballs fall out of your head?

Would You Rather...

Your mom put a basin over your head to cut your hair into that shape

OR

have your hair cut by someone with really foul disgusting breath?

Have a purple tongue like a giraffe

OR

a mask around your eyes like a raccoon?

Would You Rather...

Wear wet pants all day

OR

pants that belong to someone else?

• • • • • • • • • • • • • • •

Have purple earwax

OR

blue boogers?

Would You Rather...

Chew on a color crayon

OR

suck on a piece of chalk?

Drink a glass full of someone's sweat

OR

eat a plate of someone's eye boogers?

Would You Rather...

Sleep all night with a zombie dog beside you

OR

not sleep at all for the rest of your life?

Have two horns on your head

OR

a tail in between your legs?

Would You Rather...

Have a bunch of snails in your lunch box

OR

eat a sandwich with just one dead snail in it?

Have itchy scaly skin

OR

have oozy pus-filled blisters all over your left hand?

Would You Rather...

Be a vampire who bites people with their fangs

OR

a zombie who sucks out human brains?

• •

Have a big green wart on the side of your nose

OR

have a big shiny bald spot on the top of your head?

Would You Rather...

Dive into a pool full of zombie guts

OR

float carefully on top of a giant stinging jellyfish?

Run away from zombies thirsty for your brain

OR

from a pack of hungry wolves who want to tear you apart?

Would You Rather...

Be in a classroom with zombies

OR

a classroom with vampires?

Stay in a motel room that is dirty but smells nice

OR

in a motel that smells bad but is clean?

Would You Rather...

Run barefoot on a road filled with nails

OR

run with slippers in a road of large tarantulas?

Have someone's ear sewn in place of your ear

OR

have someone else's eyes?

Would You Rather...

Bite into a raw onion like an apple

OR

only be able to use one teaspoon of liquid dish soap to wash all the dishes in your house for a week?

Be put in a cage with chomping crocodiles

OR

in a cage with smelly baboons?

Would You Rather...

Eat lunch in the school bathroom

OR

get a drink of water from someone's sweaty gym clothes?

• • • • • • • • • • • • • • • •

Enter a haunted graveyard during the day

OR

a graveyard without ghosts in the middle of the night?

Would You Rather...

Wear a skunk skin hat

OR

wear a snake around your neck like a scarf?

• •

Have no hair on your body

OR

have hair growing out of every place on your body?

Would You Rather...

Have the forked tongue of a snake

OR

the long trunk of an elephant?

Be naked in a pool full of cockroaches

OR

wearing clothes in a pool of dead rotten fish?

Would You Rather...

Pet a smelly skunk

OR

a hedgehog with spikes on it?

• • • • • • • • • • • • • • • • • • •

Be striped like a skunk

OR

have a red bottom like a baboon?

Would You Rather...

Have someone flick their boogers at you

OR

someone flick their sweat all over you?

Flick

One of your eyes doesn't stop watering

OR

you have the feeling of water stuck in your ears that you can't get rid of?

Would You Rather...

Have wings coming out of your back

OR

have a curly pig's tail?

- - - - - - - - - - - - - - - - - - -

Be left in a dark forest alone

OR

left in a haunted house?

Would You Rather...

Eat an ice cream cone filled with bird poop

OR

a bowl of spaghetti filled with worms?

Sit in a class full of crawling insects

OR

a class full of flying bugs?

Would You Rather...

Eat a bag full of green potato chips

OR

eat a baked potato that has sprouts all over it?

Have a pet stink bug

OR

a pet slug who leaves slime trails everywhere?

Would You Rather...

Eat a sandwich made with moldy bread

OR

drink a milkshake made with rotten milk?

Eat fluff from someone else's belly-button

OR

have someone else's scab in your sandwich?

Would You Rather...

Forget to put on pants before going to school

OR

go to school wearing your mom's bright red lipstick?

Every piece of food you eat be warm

OR

every piece of food you eat be cold?

Would You Rather...

Have your friend blow their nose into your sleeve

OR

brush your hair with a comb made from insect legs?

Have a ten-inch belly-button that sways with music

OR

be constantly sticky all over?

Would You Rather...

Wear a pair of sneakers with a giant hole in the toe

OR

wear a pair of mittens in the winter with no thumb hole?

• • • • • • • • • • • • • • • • •

Have your armpit make a farting sound every time you raise your hand in class

OR

get a very loud case of the hiccups every time you don't know the answer in class?

Would You Rather...

Eat a cheeseburger with a slice of stinky cheese on it

OR

eat a hotdog that fell on the floor and now has fuzzies on it?

• • • • • • • • • • • • • • • • • • •

Only eat mayonnaise for the rest of your life

OR

when you're nervous sweat mayonnaise?

Would You Rather...

Snort like a pig every time you laugh

OR

shoot confetti from your fingertips every time you clap your hands?

Have a tick stuck in your ear

OR

a spider stuck in your nose?

Would You Rather...

Have a nose that won't stop running

OR

feet that won't stop sweating?

• • • • • • • • • • • • • • • • •

Have your butt crack showing all day at school

OR

have a long piece of toilet paper stuck to your shoe all day?

Would You Rather...

Peel an orange and eat the orange peel

OR

walk around all day with your eyes taped open?

• • • • • • • • • • • • • • • • • • • •

Swim in elephant dung

OR

swim in a stinky pond full of algae?

Would You Rather...

Leave a wet spot of sweat on every place you sit

OR

have a cloud of dirt follow you wherever you walk?

Have a huge, hairy, but non-poisonous tarantula crawling up your arm

OR

swing across the monkey bars with poisonous snakes below you?

Would You Rather...

Accidentally fall into a trash can

OR

accidentally step in a dirty bucket of mop water?

• • • • • • • • • • • • • • • • • • • •

Have your friends hear your tone-deaf mom singing loud

OR

have your friends see your dorky dad dancing?

Would You Rather...

Sleep in the same bed with someone who snores loudly

OR

sleep on a pillow with someone else's drool on it?

Eat gum from the bottom of your desk

OR

chew on the eraser of your friend's pencil?

Would You Rather...

Take a shower every day but wear dirty clothes

OR

go un-showered for weeks but have clean clothes to wear?

Have your mom or dad call you by your super-secret embarrassing nickname in front of your friends

OR

have your friends say your most super embarrassing secret in front of your parents?

Would You Rather...

Eat hot pepper pancakes

OR

peanut butter flavored cheese pizza crust?

Have clothes that look clean but stink bad

OR

have clothes that look dirty but smell super clean?

Would You Rather...

Get a big piece of gum stuck in your hair

OR

have a spider make a web in your mouth?

· ·

Roll around in wet cement

OR

muddy sand?

Would You Rather...

Wear big shiny rain boots to the beach

OR

wear a pair of flip flops in the deep snow?

• • • • • • • • • • • • • • • • • • •

Color with smelly markers that all smell like dirty feet

OR

write with pencils that smell like sweaty armpits?

Would You Rather...

Eat a moldy banana

OR

a rotten fish?

• •

Eat a package of cookies that was run over by a car

OR

a chocolate cake that fell into your kitchen sink?

Would You Rather...

Eat a half-eaten donut you find on the sidewalk

OR

put on headphones that have someone else's earwax all over them?

• • • • • • • • • • • • • • • • • • •

Pick up food scraps from the cafeteria floor with your hands

OR

pull gum from the bottom of desks with your teeth?

Would You Rather...

Wash your hair with mashed potatoes

OR

wash your body with a sponge with someone else's hair on it?

• • • • • • • • • • • • • • • • • • • •

Have hairy knuckles on your hands

OR

feet covered with llama fur?

Would You Rather...

Have a thumb that is an eraser

OR

a nose that is a pencil?

Find a random hair on your food at lunch

OR

find a crawling bug in your dessert?

Would You Rather...

Wear a permanent marker mustache

OR

have dog hair glued on your face for a beard?

• •

Sleep alone in a haunted house

OR

in a lifeboat in the middle of the ocean?

Would You Rather...

Chew on a used doggie bone

OR

chase a ball of yarn around all day?

• • • • • • • • • • • • • • • • • •

Have an itch that you cannot scratch

OR

a splinter that you cannot remove from your finger?

Would You Rather...

Eat chicken fingers made from chicken feet

OR

eat hot dogs made from real dogs?

• •

Eat macaroni and cheese made from fingernail clippings

OR

eat a cupcake with eyelash sprinkles?

Would You Rather...

Eat a mushroom sandwich

OR

pickle pancakes?

Drive on a muddy road with the windows down

OR

in a jungle with wild animals right beside your jeep?

Would You Rather...

Live in a birdhouse

OR

get your foot caught in a mouse trap?

Get to school by crawling like a baby

OR

being walked on a leash like a dog?

Would You Rather...

Have a dead parrot as your pet

OR

an anaconda?

- - - - - - - - - - - - - - - - - - -

Chew on tasteless bubblegum all your life

OR

broccoli flavored bubble gum?

Would You Rather...

Have bad diarrhea during a school presentation

OR

have uncontrollable farts?

Be locked in your school's gym with all of the smelly shirts

OR

the school cafeteria with all of the stinky food scraps?

Would You Rather...

Sleep in a room covered in dusty, sticky cobwebs

OR

sleep in a room with creeping lizards?

Have a backpack made from a cow's stomach

OR

a pencil case made from a kangaroo's pouch?

Would You Rather...

Poke someone in the eye

OR

have someone poke you in the eye?

Be locked in a room full of flying birds and feathers

OR

crawling insects with random legs falling off?

Would You Rather...

Lose your talking voice and only be able to sing

OR

lose your sight only when you watch TV or play video games?

• • • • • • • • • • • • • • • • • • • •

Eat food that is dripping with grease

OR

drink milk with chunks of cottage cheese in it?

Would You Rather...

Have big zits all over your body

OR

just one big one on your nose?

• •

Pee on someone who has been stung by a jellyfish

OR

have someone pee on you after you've been stung by a jellyfish?

Would You Rather...

Be stung by a bee on the nose

OR

bitten by an ant on the toe?

• • • • • • • • • • • • • • • • •

Have a giant spider walk all over your body

OR

an oozing slug crawl on you?

Would You Rather...

Let a cat lick you dry after a shower

OR

use sandpaper to file your nails?

Find your kitchen covered in grime

OR

your house covered in mold?

Would You Rather...

Sleep in a bed full of cracker crumbs

OR

use a bag of potato chips as your pillow?

Take a bath in your boogers every day

OR

take a bath in someone else's boogers just once?

Would You Rather...

Burp whenever you cry

OR

fart whenever you laugh?

See laser-shooting rainbow kitties wherever you look

OR

confetti sprinkling battle unicorns whenever you close your eyes?

Would You Rather...

Be caught wearing a diaper under your pants

OR

shopping at the store carrying your grandma's purse?

Have a large cobweb brush against your face

OR

have a tarantula climb up your arm?

Would You Rather...

Wash someone's dirty shoes by hand

OR

wash someone's dirty socks?

• • • • • • • • • • • • • • • • • • • •

Accidentally belly flop into the pool in front of your friends

OR

accidentally trip down the stairs in front of the whole school?

Would You Rather...

Find a long dark piece of hair in your cafeteria food

OR

find a moldy piece of fruit in your fruit salad?

- - -

Scrub the tiles of a public toilet

OR

scrub the floor of your bathroom using a dirty scrubber?

Would You Rather...

Have multiple paper cuts all over your body

OR

scrape both of your knees ?

- - - - - - - - - - - - - - -

Sprain your ankle during a dance rehearsal

OR

fall off a bike and scratch your elbows?

Would You Rather...

Eat ice cubes made from frozen cooking oil

OR

ice cubes made from melted butter?

Jump in a bouncy house with your bare, stinky feet

OR

swing from the monkey bars in a tank top with really stinky armpits?

Would You Rather...

Have a giant watermelon-sized head

OR

a tiny tennis-ball-sized head?

• • • • • • • • • • • • • • • • • • • •

Have a pimple burst and spray people near to you with pus every time you speak

OR

snot come out of your nose every time you laugh?

Would You Rather...

Eat an apple with worms in it

OR

salad with caterpillars in it?

Have someone pull out your broken nail

OR

pull out a kind of wiggly tooth?

Would You Rather...

Eat stale bread for the rest of your life

OR

rotten eggs every day?

• •

Eat cereal out of a fishbowl

OR

popcorn out of a hamster cage?

Would You Rather...

Decorate your room with spiderwebs

OR

sleep wrapped in a butterfly cocoon?

Eat a large plate of mashed Brussels sprouts

OR

eat a large bowl of Semolina?

Would You Rather...

Wear itchy clothes that are too short

OR

wear slimy clothes that are too large for your size?

• • • • • • • • • • • • • • • • • • • •

Have a friend that smells bad, and you have to smell them all the time

OR

have no friends at all?

104

Would You Rather...

Be friends with someone who never brushes their teeth

OR

someone who never showers?

Clean the floor of a school bus

OR

pick up litter off a beach to clean it?

Would You Rather...

Eat a whole stick of butter with your hands

OR

eat an entire jar of mayonnaise with a straw?

Be showered by slobbering dog drool
as a dog shakes its head near you

OR

be clambered on by a puppy who has just rolled
in something smelly?

Would You Rather...

Believe you are a real superhero but have no powers

OR

be a real superhero with a super case of body odor?

Swim in a pool of sourdough starter

OR

eat a whole bowl of stinky tofu?

Would You Rather...

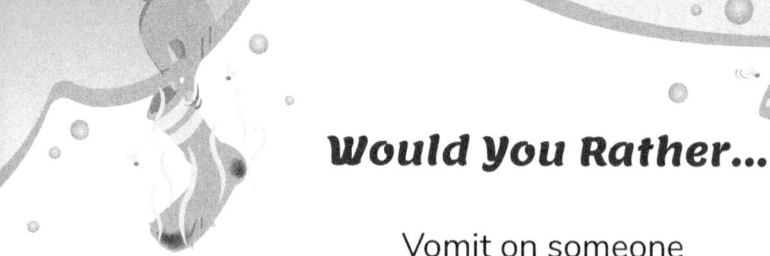

Vomit on someone

OR

have someone vomit on you?

Step on a slug in bare feet

OR

find a half eaten worm in your apple after your first bite?

Did You Enjoy The Book ?

If you did, we are ecstatic. If not, please write your complaint to us and we will ensure we fix it.

If you're feeling generous, there is something important that you can help me with – tell other people that you enjoyed the book.

Ask a grown-up to write about it on Amazon. When they do, more people will find out about the book. It also lets Amazon know that we are making kids around the world enjoy reading and asking and answering 'Would you rather ...' questions. Even a few words and ratings would go a long way.

If you have any ideas or Would you rather ... questions that you think are interesting, please let us know. We would love to hear from you.

Our email address is -
riddleland@riddlelandforkids.com

Riddleland Bonus

Join our **Facebook Group** at **Riddleland for Kids**
to get daily jokes and riddles.

https://pixelfy.me/riddlelandbonus

Thank you for buying this book. As a token of our appreciation, we would like to offer a special bonus—a collection of 50 original jokes, riddles, and funny stories.

CONTEST

Would you like your jokes and riddles to be featured in our next book?

We are having a contest to discover the cleverest and funniest boys and girls in the world!

1) Creative and Challenging Riddles
2) Tickle Your Funny Bone Contest

Parents, please email us your child's "original" riddle or joke. He or she could win a Riddleland book and be featured in our next book.

Here are the rules:

1) We're looking for super challenging riddles and extra funny jokes.

2) Jokes and riddles MUST be 100% original—NOT something discovered on the Internet.

3) You can submit both a joke and a riddle because they are two separate contests.

4) Don't get help from your parents—UNLESS they're as funny as you are.

5) Winners will be announced via email or our Facebook group – **Riddleland for kids**

6) In your entry, please confirm which book you purchased.

Email us at **Riddleland@riddlelandforkids.com**

Other Fun Books by Riddleland
Riddles Series

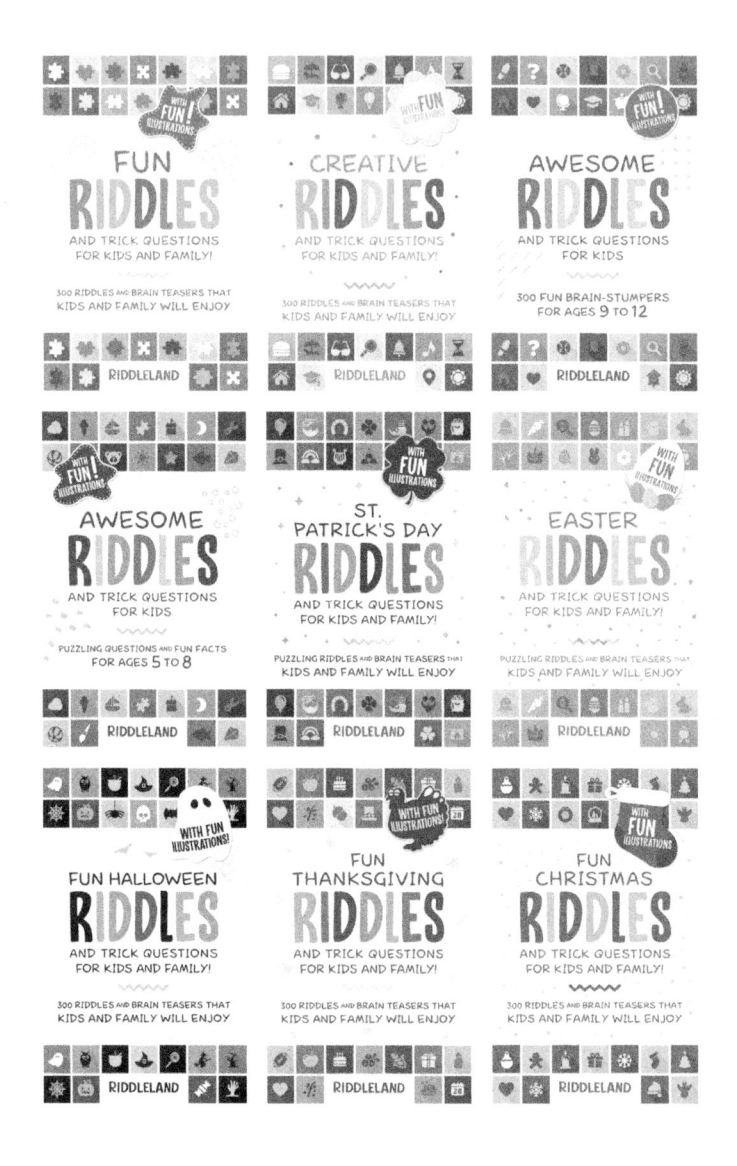

Would You Rather...Series

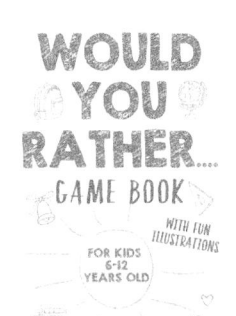

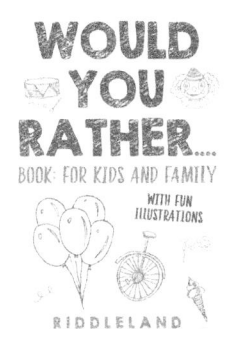

Get them on Amazon or our website at
www.riddlelandforkids.com

ABOUT RIDDLELAND

Riddleland is a mum + dad run publishing company. We are passionate about creating fun and innovative books to help children develop their reading skills and fall in love with reading. If you have suggestions for us or want to work with us, shoot us an email at

riddleland@riddlelandforkids.com

Our favourite family quote

"Creativity is an area in which younger people have a tremendous advantage since they have an endearing habit of always questioning past wisdom and authority."

– Bill Hewlett

Printed in Great Britain
by Amazon